D0942983

Travel Log

KNOCK
KNOCK®
VENICE, CALIFORNIA

Created and published by Knock Knock
Distributed by Who's There Inc.
Venice, CA 90291
knockknockstuff.com

ISBN: 978-160106305-2
UPC: 8-25703-15139-8

10 9 8 7 6 5 4 3 2 1

WHETHER YOU'RE AN INCESSANT GLOBE-TROTTER OR AN ARMCHAIR TRAVELER, CONTEMPLATING ONE'S next trip is a thoroughly delightful experience. Inspiration may strike at any time or any place. Will you be ready? Fortunately, the Travel Log is a comprehensive and portable—dare we say travel-sized?—repository for all your travel aspirations, plans, and experiences. Muse about your latest dream destination, organize the perfect itinerary, and record the indelible memories that are bound to follow. Now, whenever and wherever your wanderlust wanders, you'll be on the go *and* in the know as you manage your adventures in style.

Inspiration

INSPIRATION

DREAM DESTINATION:

SOURCE: ☐ BOOK ☐ MAGAZINE ☐ WEB ☐ OTHER _____

REASON:

☐ FIND SELF
☐ LOSE SELF

NOT TO MISS

1.

2.

3.

4.

5.

6.

7.

8.

NOTES:

☐ INSPIRED

DREAM DESTINATION:

SOURCE: ☐ BOOK ☐ MAGAZINE
☐ WEB ☐ OTHER _____

REASON:

☐ FIND SELF
☐ LOSE SELF

NOT TO MISS

1.

2.

3.

4.

5.

6.

7.

8.

NOTES:

☐ INSPIRED

INSPIRATION

DREAM DESTINATION:

SOURCE:
☐ BOOK ☐ MAGAZINE
☐ WEB ☐ OTHER _____

REASON:

☐ FIND SELF
☐ LOSE SELF

NOT TO MISS

1.

2.

3.

4.

5.

6.

7.

8.

NOTES:

☐ INSPIRED

DREAM DESTINATION:

SOURCE:
☐ BOOK ☐ MAGAZINE
☐ WEB ☐ OTHER _____

REASON:

☐ FIND SELF
☐ LOSE SELF

NOT TO MISS

1.
2.
3.
4.
5.
6.
7.
8.

NOTES:

☐ INSPIRED

INSPIRATION

DREAM DESTINATION:

SOURCE: ☐ BOOK ☐ MAGAZINE
☐ WEB ☐ OTHER _____

REASON:

☐ FIND SELF
☐ LOSE SELF

NOT TO MISS

1.

2.

3.

4.

5.

6.

7.

8.

NOTES:

☐ INSPIRED

DREAM DESTINATION:

SOURCE:

☐ BOOK ☐ MAGAZINE
☐ WEB ☐ OTHER _____

REASON:

☐ FIND SELF
☐ LOSE SELF

NOT TO MISS

1.

2.

3.

4.

5.

6.

7.

8.

NOTES:

☐ INSPIRED

INSPIRATION

DREAM DESTINATION:

SOURCE: ☐ BOOK ☐ MAGAZINE
☐ WEB ☐ OTHER _____

REASON:

☐ FIND SELF
☐ LOSE SELF

NOT TO MISS

1.
2.
3.
4.
5.
6.
7.
8.

NOTES:

☐ INSPIRED

DREAM DESTINATION:

SOURCE: ☐ BOOK ☐ MAGAZINE
☐ WEB ☐ OTHER _____

REASON:

☐ FIND SELF
☐ LOSE SELF

NOT TO MISS

1.

2.

3.

4.

5.

6.

7.

8.

NOTES:

☐ INSPIRED

INSPIRATION

DREAM DESTINATION:

SOURCE: ☐ BOOK ☐ MAGAZINE ☐ WEB ☐ OTHER _____

REASON:

☐ FIND SELF
☐ LOSE SELF

NOT TO MISS

1.

2.

3.

4.

5.

6.

7.

8.

NOTES:

☐ INSPIRED

DREAM DESTINATION:

SOURCE: ☐ BOOK ☐ MAGAZINE
☐ WEB ☐ OTHER _____

REASON:

_____

_____

_____

_____

_____

☐ FIND SELF
☐ LOSE SELF

NOT TO MISS

1. _____

2. _____

3. _____

4. _____

5. _____

6. _____

7. _____

8. _____

NOTES:

_____

_____

_____

_____

_____

_____

☐ INSPIRED

INSPIRATION

DREAM DESTINATION:

SOURCE:
☐ BOOK ☐ MAGAZINE
☐ WEB ☐ OTHER _____

REASON:

☐ FIND SELF
☐ LOSE SELF

NOT TO MISS

1.

2.

3.

4.

5.

6.

7.

8.

NOTES:

☐ INSPIRED

DREAM DESTINATION:

SOURCE: ☐ BOOK ☐ MAGAZINE
☐ WEB ☐ OTHER _____

REASON:

☐ FIND SELF
☐ LOSE SELF

NOT TO MISS

1.
2.
3.
4.
5.
6.
7.
8.

NOTES:

☐ INSPIRED

INSPIRATION

DREAM DESTINATION:

SOURCE: ☐ BOOK ☐ MAGAZINE
☐ WEB ☐ OTHER _____

REASON:

☐ FIND SELF
☐ LOSE SELF

NOT TO MISS

1.

2.

3.

4.

5.

6.

7.

8.

NOTES:

☐ INSPIRED

DREAM DESTINATION:

SOURCE: ☐ BOOK ☐ MAGAZINE ☐ WEB ☐ OTHER _____

REASON:

_____

_____

_____

_____

☐ FIND SELF
☐ LOSE SELF

NOT TO MISS

1. _____

2. _____

3. _____

4. _____

5. _____

6. _____

7. _____

8. _____

NOTES:

_____

_____

_____

_____

_____

_____

☐ INSPIRED

INSPIRATION

DREAM DESTINATION:

SOURCE: ☐ BOOK ☐ MAGAZINE
☐ WEB ☐ OTHER _____

REASON:

☐ FIND SELF
☐ LOSE SELF

NOT TO MISS

1.
2.
3.
4.
5.
6.
7.
8.

NOTES:

☐ INSPIRED

DREAM DESTINATION:

SOURCE:
☐ BOOK ☐ MAGAZINE
☐ WEB ☐ OTHER _____

REASON:

☐ FIND SELF
☐ LOSE SELF

NOT TO MISS

1.

2.

3.

4.

5.

6.

7.

8.

NOTES:

☐ INSPIRED

INSPIRATION

DREAM DESTINATION:

SOURCE: ☐ BOOK ☐ MAGAZINE
☐ WEB ☐ OTHER _____

REASON:

☐ FIND SELF
☐ LOSE SELF

NOT TO MISS

1.

2.

3.

4.

5.

6.

7.

8.

NOTES:

☐ INSPIRED

DREAM DESTINATION:

SOURCE: ☐ BOOK ☐ MAGAZINE
              ☐ WEB ☐ OTHER _____

REASON:

☐ FIND SELF
☐ LOSE SELF

NOT TO MISS

1.
2.
3.
4.
5.
6.
7.
8.

NOTES:

☐ INSPIRED

INSPIRATION

DREAM DESTINATION:

SOURCE: ☐ BOOK ☐ MAGAZINE ☐ WEB ☐ OTHER _____

REASON:

☐ FIND SELF
☐ LOSE SELF

NOT TO MISS

1.

2.

3.

4.

5.

6.

7.

8.

NOTES:

☐ INSPIRED

DREAM DESTINATION:

SOURCE:
☐ BOOK ☐ MAGAZINE
☐ WEB ☐ OTHER _____

REASON:

☐ FIND SELF
☐ LOSE SELF

NOT TO MISS

1.

2.

3.

4.

5.

6.

7.

8.

NOTES:

☐ INSPIRED

INSPIRATION

DREAM DESTINATION:

SOURCE: ☐ BOOK ☐ MAGAZINE ☐ WEB ☐ OTHER _____

REASON:

☐ FIND SELF
☐ LOSE SELF

NOT TO MISS

1.
2.
3.
4.
5.
6.
7.
8.

NOTES:

☐ INSPIRED

DREAM DESTINATION:

SOURCE: ☐ BOOK ☐ MAGAZINE
☐ WEB ☐ OTHER _____

REASON:

☐ FIND SELF
☐ LOSE SELF

NOT TO MISS

1.
2.
3.
4.
5.
6.
7.
8.

NOTES:

☐ INSPIRED

INSPIRATION

DREAM DESTINATION:

SOURCE: ☐ BOOK ☐ MAGAZINE
☐ WEB ☐ OTHER _____

REASON:

☐ FIND SELF
☐ LOSE SELF

NOT TO MISS

1.

2.

3.

4.

5.

6.

7.

8.

NOTES:

☐ INSPIRED

DREAM DESTINATION:

SOURCE:

☐ BOOK ☐ MAGAZINE
☐ WEB ☐ OTHER _____

REASON:

☐ FIND SELF
☐ LOSE SELF

NOT TO MISS

1.
2.
3.
4.
5.
6.
7.
8.

NOTES:

☐ INSPIRED

INSPIRATION

DREAM DESTINATION:

SOURCE: ☐ BOOK ☐ MAGAZINE
☐ WEB ☐ OTHER _____

REASON:

☐ FIND SELF
☐ LOSE SELF

NOT TO MISS

1.
2.
3.
4.
5.
6.
7.
8.

NOTES:

☐ INSPIRED

DREAM DESTINATION:

SOURCE: ☐ BOOK ☐ MAGAZINE
☐ WEB ☐ OTHER _____

REASON:

☐ FIND SELF
☐ LOSE SELF

NOT TO MISS

1.
2.
3.
4.
5.
6.
7.
8.

NOTES:

☐ INSPIRED

INSPIRATION

DREAM DESTINATION:

SOURCE:
☐ BOOK ☐ MAGAZINE
☐ WEB ☐ OTHER _____

REASON:

☐ FIND SELF
☐ LOSE SELF

NOT TO MISS

1.

2.

3.

4.

5.

6.

7.

8.

NOTES:

☐ INSPIRED

DREAM DESTINATION:

SOURCE: ☐ BOOK ☐ MAGAZINE
☐ WEB ☐ OTHER _____

REASON:

☐ FIND SELF
☐ LOSE SELF

NOT TO MISS

1.

2.

3.

4.

5.

6.

7.

8.

NOTES:

☐ INSPIRED

INSPIRATION

DREAM DESTINATION:

SOURCE: ☐ BOOK ☐ MAGAZINE
☐ WEB ☐ OTHER _____

REASON:

☐ FIND SELF
☐ LOSE SELF

NOT TO MISS

1.
2.
3.
4.
5.
6.
7.
8.

NOTES:

☐ INSPIRED

DREAM DESTINATION:

SOURCE: ☐ BOOK ☐ MAGAZINE
☐ WEB ☐ OTHER _____

REASON:

☐ FIND SELF
☐ LOSE SELF

NOT TO MISS

1.

2.

3.

4.

5.

6.

7.

8.

NOTES:

☐ INSPIRED

INSPIRATION

DREAM DESTINATION:

SOURCE:
☐ BOOK ☐ MAGAZINE
☐ WEB ☐ OTHER _____

REASON:

☐ FIND SELF
☐ LOSE SELF

NOT TO MISS

1.
2.
3.
4.
5.
6.
7.
8.

NOTES:

☐ INSPIRED

DREAM DESTINATION:

SOURCE: ☐ BOOK ☐ MAGAZINE
☐ WEB ☐ OTHER _____

REASON:

☐ FIND SELF
☐ LOSE SELF

NOT TO MISS

1.
2.
3.
4.
5.
6.
7.
8.

NOTES:

☐ INSPIRED

INSPIRATION

DREAM DESTINATION:

SOURCE: ☐ BOOK ☐ MAGAZINE
☐ WEB ☐ OTHER _____

REASON:

☐ FIND SELF
☐ LOSE SELF

NOT TO MISS

1.
2.
3.
4.
5.
6.
7.
8.

NOTES:

☐ INSPIRED

DREAM DESTINATION:

SOURCE: ☐ BOOK ☐ MAGAZINE
☐ WEB ☐ OTHER _____

REASON:

_____

_____

_____

_____

☐ FIND SELF
☐ LOSE SELF

NOT TO MISS

1.

2.

3.

4.

5.

6.

7.

8.

NOTES:

_____

_____

_____

_____

_____

_____

☐ **INSPIRED**

INSPIRATION

DREAM DESTINATION:

SOURCE: ☐ BOOK ☐ MAGAZINE ☐ WEB ☐ OTHER _____

REASON:

☐ FIND SELF
☐ LOSE SELF

NOT TO MISS

1.
2.
3.
4.
5.
6.
7.
8.

NOTES:

☐ INSPIRED

DREAM DESTINATION:

SOURCE: ☐ BOOK ☐ MAGAZINE ☐ WEB ☐ OTHER _____

REASON:

☐ FIND SELF
☐ LOSE SELF

NOT TO MISS

1.

2.

3.

4.

5.

6.

7.

8.

NOTES:

☐ INSPIRED

planning

TRIP:

TRAVEL COMPANION(S):

TRANSPORTATION

☐ PLANE   ☐ TRAIN   ☐ AUTO   ☐ BUS   ☐ BOAT   ☐ OTHER

CARRIER:

DEPARTURE DATE: /   /   ARRIVAL DATE: /   /

CONF. No.:

DETAILS:

LODGING

NAME:

CONTACT INFO:

CONF. No.:

DETAILS:

EXCURSIONS/ACTIVITIES

☐ PLANNED

TRIP:

TRAVEL COMPANION(S):

TRANSPORTATION

□ PLANE   □ TRAIN   □ AUTO   □ BUS   □ BOAT   □ OTHER

CARRIER:

DEPARTURE DATE: /   /   **ARRIVAL DATE:**   /   /

CONF. No.:

DETAILS:

LODGING

NAME:

CONTACT INFO:

CONF. No.:

DETAILS:

EXCURSIONS/ACTIVITIES

□ PLANNED

TRIP:

TRAVEL COMPANION(S):

TRANSPORTATION

☐ PLANE ☐ TRAIN ☐ AUTO ☐ BUS ☐ BOAT ☐ OTHER

CARRIER:

DEPARTURE DATE: / /	ARRIVAL DATE: / /

CONF. No.:

DETAILS:

LODGING

NAME:

CONTACT INFO:

CONF. No.:

DETAILS:

EXCURSIONS/ACTIVITIES

☐ PLANNED

TRIP:

TRAVEL COMPANION(S):

TRANSPORTATION

☐ PLANE ☐ TRAIN ☐ AUTO ☐ BUS ☐ BOAT ☐ OTHER

CARRIER:

DEPARTURE DATE: / / ARRIVAL DATE: / /

CONF. No.:

DETAILS:

LODGING

NAME:

CONTACT INFO:

CONF. No.:

DETAILS:

EXCURSIONS/ACTIVITIES

☐ PLANNED

PLANNING

TRIP:

TRAVEL COMPANION(S):

TRANSPORTATION

☐ PLANE   ☐ TRAIN   ☐ AUTO   ☐ BUS   ☐ BOAT   ☐ OTHER

CARRIER:

| **DEPARTURE DATE:**   /   / | **ARRIVAL DATE:**   /   / |

CONF. No.:

DETAILS:

LODGING

NAME:

CONTACT INFO:

CONF. No.:

DETAILS:

EXCURSIONS/ACTIVITIES

☐ PLANNED

TRIP:

TRAVEL COMPANION(S):

TRANSPORTATION

☐ PLANE   ☐ TRAIN   ☐ AUTO   ☐ BUS   ☐ BOAT   ☐ OTHER

CARRIER:

DEPARTURE DATE: /   /   **ARRIVAL DATE:**   /   /

CONF. No.:

DETAILS:

LODGING

NAME:

CONTACT INFO:

CONF. No.:

DETAILS:

EXCURSIONS/ACTIVITIES

☐ PLANNED

PLANNING

TRIP:

TRAVEL COMPANION(S):

TRANSPORTATION

□ PLANE　　□ TRAIN　　□ AUTO　　□ BUS　　□ BOAT　　□ OTHER

CARRIER:

DEPARTURE DATE:　　/　　/　　　　ARRIVAL DATE:　　/　　/

CONF. No.:

DETAILS:

LODGING

NAME:

CONTACT INFO:

CONF. No.:

DETAILS:

EXCURSIONS/ACTIVITIES

□ PLANNED

TRIP:

TRAVEL COMPANION(S):

TRANSPORTATION

☐ PLANE ☐ TRAIN ☐ AUTO ☐ BUS ☐ BOAT ☐ OTHER

CARRIER:

DEPARTURE DATE: / / **ARRIVAL DATE:** / /

CONF. No.:

DETAILS:

LODGING

NAME:

CONTACT INFO:

CONF. No.:

DETAILS:

EXCURSIONS/ACTIVITIES

☐ PLANNED

TRIP:

TRAVEL COMPANION(S):

TRANSPORTATION

☐ PLANE ☐ TRAIN ☐ AUTO ☐ BUS ☐ BOAT ☐ OTHER

CARRIER:

DEPARTURE DATE: / / **ARRIVAL DATE:** / /

CONF. No.:

DETAILS:

LODGING

NAME:

CONTACT INFO:

CONF. No.:

DETAILS:

EXCURSIONS/ACTIVITIES

☐ PLANNED

TRIP:

TRAVEL COMPANION(S):

TRANSPORTATION

☐ PLANE ☐ TRAIN ☐ AUTO ☐ BUS ☐ BOAT ☐ OTHER

CARRIER:

DEPARTURE DATE: / /   **ARRIVAL DATE:** / /

CONF. No.:

DETAILS:

LODGING

NAME:

CONTACT INFO:

CONF. No.:

DETAILS:

EXCURSIONS/ACTIVITIES

☐ PLANNED

PLANNING

TRIP:

TRAVEL COMPANION(S):

TRANSPORTATION

☐ PLANE   ☐ TRAIN   ☐ AUTO   ☐ BUS   ☐ BOAT   ☐ OTHER

CARRIER:

DEPARTURE DATE: /   /   ARRIVAL DATE: /   /

CONF. No.:

DETAILS:

LODGING

NAME:

CONTACT INFO:

CONF. No.:

DETAILS:

EXCURSIONS/ACTIVITIES

☐ PLANNED

TRIP:

TRAVEL COMPANION(S):

TRANSPORTATION

☐ PLANE ☐ TRAIN ☐ AUTO ☐ BUS ☐ BOAT ☐ OTHER

CARRIER:

DEPARTURE DATE: / / **ARRIVAL DATE:** / /

CONF. No.:

DETAILS:

LODGING

NAME:

CONTACT INFO:

CONF. No.:

DETAILS:

EXCURSIONS/ACTIVITIES

☐ PLANNED

TRIP:

TRAVEL COMPANION(S):

TRANSPORTATION

☐ PLANE   ☐ TRAIN   ☐ AUTO   ☐ BUS   ☐ BOAT   ☐ OTHER

CARRIER:

DEPARTURE DATE: /   / | ARRIVAL DATE: /   /

CONF. No.:

DETAILS:

LODGING

NAME:

CONTACT INFO:

CONF. No.:

DETAILS:

EXCURSIONS/ACTIVITIES

☐ PLANNED

TRIP:

TRAVEL COMPANION(S):

TRANSPORTATION

☐ PLANE ☐ TRAIN ☐ AUTO ☐ BUS ☐ BOAT ☐ OTHER

CARRIER:

DEPARTURE DATE: / / **ARRIVAL DATE:** / /

CONF. No.:

DETAILS:

LODGING

NAME:

CONTACT INFO:

CONF. No.:

DETAILS:

EXCURSIONS/ACTIVITIES

☐ PLANNED

TRIP:

TRAVEL COMPANION(S):

TRANSPORTATION

☐ PLANE   ☐ TRAIN   ☐ AUTO   ☐ BUS   ☐ BOAT   ☐ OTHER

CARRIER:

DEPARTURE DATE: /   /   ARRIVAL DATE: /   /

CONF. No.:

DETAILS:

LODGING

NAME:

CONTACT INFO:

CONF. No.:

DETAILS:

EXCURSIONS/ACTIVITIES

☐ PLANNED

TRIP:

TRAVEL COMPANION(S):

TRANSPORTATION

☐ PLANE ☐ TRAIN ☐ AUTO ☐ BUS ☐ BOAT ☐ OTHER

CARRIER:

DEPARTURE DATE: / /   **ARRIVAL DATE:** / /

CONF. No.:

DETAILS:

LODGING

NAME:

CONTACT INFO:

CONF. No.:

DETAILS:

EXCURSIONS/ACTIVITIES

☐ PLANNED

PLANNING

TRIP:

TRAVEL COMPANION(S):

TRANSPORTATION

☐ PLANE ☐ TRAIN ☐ AUTO ☐ BUS ☐ BOAT ☐ OTHER

CARRIER:

DEPARTURE DATE: /   /   ARRIVAL DATE: /   /

CONF. No.:

DETAILS:

LODGING

NAME:

CONTACT INFO:

CONF. No.:

DETAILS:

EXCURSIONS/ACTIVITIES

☐ PLANNED

TRIP:

TRAVEL COMPANION(S):

TRANSPORTATION

☐ PLANE   ☐ TRAIN   ☐ AUTO   ☐ BUS   ☐ BOAT   ☐ OTHER

CARRIER:

DEPARTURE DATE: /   /   **ARRIVAL DATE:**   /   /

CONF. No.:

DETAILS:

LODGING

NAME:

CONTACT INFO:

CONF. No.:

DETAILS:

EXCURSIONS/ACTIVITIES

☐ PLANNED

TRIP:

TRAVEL COMPANION(S):

TRANSPORTATION

☐ PLANE   ☐ TRAIN   ☐ AUTO   ☐ BUS   ☐ BOAT   ☐ OTHER

CARRIER:

DEPARTURE DATE: /   /   ARRIVAL DATE: /   /

CONF. No.:

DETAILS:

LODGING

NAME:

CONTACT INFO:

CONF. No.:

DETAILS:

EXCURSIONS/ACTIVITIES

☐ PLANNED

TRIP:

TRAVEL COMPANION(S):

TRANSPORTATION

☐ PLANE ☐ TRAIN ☐ AUTO ☐ BUS ☐ BOAT ☐ OTHER

CARRIER:

DEPARTURE DATE: / / **ARRIVAL DATE:** / /

CONF. No.:

DETAILS:

LODGING

NAME:

CONTACT INFO:

CONF. No.:

DETAILS:

EXCURSIONS/ACTIVITIES

☐ PLANNED

PLANNING

TRIP:

TRAVEL COMPANION(S):

TRANSPORTATION

☐ PLANE   ☐ TRAIN   ☐ AUTO   ☐ BUS   ☐ BOAT   ☐ OTHER

CARRIER:

DEPARTURE DATE: / /	ARRIVAL DATE: / /

CONF. No.:

DETAILS:

LODGING

NAME:

CONTACT INFO:

CONF. No.:

DETAILS:

EXCURSIONS/ACTIVITIES

☐ PLANNED

TRIP:

TRAVEL COMPANION(S):

TRANSPORTATION

☐ PLANE　　☐ TRAIN　　☐ AUTO　　☐ BUS　　☐ BOAT　　☐ OTHER

CARRIER:

DEPARTURE DATE:　　/　　/　　　　**ARRIVAL DATE:**　　/　　/

CONF. No.:

DETAILS:

LODGING

NAME:

CONTACT INFO:

CONF. No.:

DETAILS:

EXCURSIONS/ACTIVITIES

☐ PLANNED

TRIP:

TRAVEL COMPANION(S):

TRANSPORTATION

☐ PLANE ☐ TRAIN ☐ AUTO ☐ BUS ☐ BOAT ☐ OTHER

CARRIER:

DEPARTURE DATE: / / ARRIVAL DATE: / /

CONF. No.:

DETAILS:

LODGING

NAME:

CONTACT INFO:

CONF. No.:

DETAILS:

EXCURSIONS/ACTIVITIES

☐ PLANNED

TRIP:

TRAVEL COMPANION(S):

TRANSPORTATION

☐ PLANE ☐ TRAIN ☐ AUTO ☐ BUS ☐ BOAT ☐ OTHER

CARRIER:

DEPARTURE DATE: / / **ARRIVAL DATE:** / /

CONF. No.:

DETAILS:

LODGING

NAME:

CONTACT INFO:

CONF. No.:

DETAILS:

EXCURSIONS/ACTIVITIES

☐ PLANNED

TRIP:

TRAVEL COMPANION(S):

TRANSPORTATION

☐ PLANE   ☐ TRAIN   ☐ AUTO   ☐ BUS   ☐ BOAT   ☐ OTHER

CARRIER:

DEPARTURE DATE: /   /   ARRIVAL DATE: /   /

CONF. No.:

DETAILS:

LODGING

NAME:

CONTACT INFO:

CONF. No.:

DETAILS:

EXCURSIONS/ACTIVITIES

☐ PLANNED

TRIP:

TRAVEL COMPANION(S):

TRANSPORTATION

☐ PLANE ☐ TRAIN ☐ AUTO ☐ BUS ☐ BOAT ☐ OTHER

CARRIER:

DEPARTURE DATE: / / **ARRIVAL DATE:** / /

CONF. No.:

DETAILS:

LODGING

NAME:

CONTACT INFO:

CONF. No.:

DETAILS:

EXCURSIONS/ACTIVITIES

☐ PLANNED

PLANNING

TRIP:

TRAVEL COMPANION(S):

TRANSPORTATION

☐ PLANE ☐ TRAIN ☐ AUTO ☐ BUS ☐ BOAT ☐ OTHER

CARRIER:

| DEPARTURE DATE: / / | ARRIVAL DATE: / / |

CONF. No.:

DETAILS:

LODGING

NAME:

CONTACT INFO·

CONF. No.:

DETAILS:

EXCURSIONS/ACTIVITIES

☐ PLANNED

TRIP:

TRAVEL COMPANION(S):

TRANSPORTATION

☐ PLANE ☐ TRAIN ☐ AUTO ☐ BUS ☐ BOAT ☐ OTHER

CARRIER:

DEPARTURE DATE: / / **ARRIVAL DATE:** / /

CONF. No.:

DETAILS:

LODGING

NAME:

CONTACT INFO:

CONF. No.:

DETAILS:

EXCURSIONS/ACTIVITIES

☐ PLANNED

TRIP:

TRAVEL COMPANION(S):

TRANSPORTATION

☐ PLANE ☐ TRAIN ☐ AUTO ☐ BUS ☐ BOAT ☐ OTHER

CARRIER:

DEPARTURE DATE: / /   ARRIVAL DATE: / /

CONF. No.:

DETAILS:

LODGING

NAME:

CONTACT INFO:

CONF. No.:

DETAILS:

EXCURSIONS/ACTIVITIES

☐ PLANNED

TRIP:

TRAVEL COMPANION(S):

TRANSPORTATION

☐ PLANE ☐ TRAIN ☐ AUTO ☐ BUS ☐ BOAT ☐ OTHER

CARRIER:

DEPARTURE DATE: / / **ARRIVAL DATE:** / /

CONF. No.:

DETAILS:

LODGING

NAME:

CONTACT INFO:

CONF. No.:

DETAILS:

EXCURSIONS/ACTIVITIES

☐ PLANNED

TRIP:

TRAVEL COMPANION(S):

TRANSPORTATION

☐ PLANE ☐ TRAIN ☐ AUTO ☐ BUS ☐ BOAT ☐ OTHER

CARRIER:

DEPARTURE DATE: / /   **ARRIVAL DATE:** / /

CONF. No.:

DETAILS:

LODGING

NAME:

CONTACT INFO:

CONF. No.:

DETAILS:

EXCURSIONS/ACTIVITIES

☐ PLANNED

TRIP:

TRAVEL COMPANION(S):

TRANSPORTATION

☐ PLANE   ☐ TRAIN   ☐ AUTO   ☐ BUS   ☐ BOAT   ☐ OTHER

CARRIER:

DEPARTURE DATE: /   /   **ARRIVAL DATE:**   /   /

CONF. No.:

DETAILS:

LODGING

NAME:

CONTACT INFO:

CONF. No.:

DETAILS:

EXCURSIONS/ACTIVITIES

☐ PLANNED

TRIP:

TRAVEL COMPANION(S):

TRANSPORTATION

☐ PLANE   ☐ TRAIN   ☐ AUTO   ☐ BUS   ☐ BOAT   ☐ OTHER

CARRIER:

DEPARTURE DATE: /   /   ARRIVAL DATE: /   /

CONF. No.:

DETAILS:

LODGING

NAME:

CONTACT INFO:

CONF. No.:

DETAILS:

EXCURSIONS/ACTIVITIES

☐ PLANNED

TRIP:

TRAVEL COMPANION(S):

TRANSPORTATION

□ PLANE   □ TRAIN   □ AUTO   □ BUS   □ BOAT   □ OTHER

CARRIER:

DEPARTURE DATE: /   /   **ARRIVAL DATE:**   /   /

CONF. No.:

DETAILS:

LODGING

NAME:

CONTACT INFO:

CONF. No.:

DETAILS:

EXCURSIONS/ACTIVITIES

□ PLANNED

TRIP:

TRAVEL COMPANION(S):

TRANSPORTATION

☐ PLANE   ☐ TRAIN   ☐ AUTO   ☐ BUS   ☐ BOAT   ☐ OTHER

CARRIER:

DEPARTURE DATE: / /	ARRIVAL DATE: / /

CONF. No.:

DETAILS:

LODGING

NAME:

CONTACT INFO:

CONF. No.:

DETAILS:

EXCURSIONS/ACTIVITIES

☐ PLANNED

TRIP: _____

TRAVEL COMPANION(S): _____

_____

TRANSPORTATION

☐ PLANE ☐ TRAIN ☐ AUTO ☐ BUS ☐ BOAT ☐ OTHER

CARRIER: _____

DEPARTURE DATE: ___ / ___ / ___   **ARRIVAL DATE:** ___ / ___ / ___

CONF. No.: _____

DETAILS: _____

_____

LODGING

NAME: _____

CONTACT INFO: _____

CONF. No.: _____

DETAILS: _____

_____

EXCURSIONS/ACTIVITIES

_____

_____

_____

_____

_____

_____

_____

☐ PLANNED

Observations

OBSERVATIONS

TRIP: DATE: /   /

LOCATION(S):

IMPRESSION(S):

NOTES/MAPS/SKETCHES:

☐ OBSERVED

TRIP:	DATE: / /

LOCATION(S):

IMPRESSION(S):

NOTES/MAPS/SKETCHES:

☐ OBSERVED

OBSERVATIONS

TRIP:	DATE: / /

LOCATION(S):

IMPRESSION(S):

NOTES/MAPS/SKETCHES:

☐ OBSERVED

TRIP:	DATE:	/	/

LOCATION(S):

IMPRESSION(S):

NOTES/MAPS/SKETCHES:

☐ OBSERVED

OBSERVATIONS

TRIP:	DATE: / /

LOCATION(S):

IMPRESSION(S):

NOTES/MAPS/SKETCHES:

☐ OBSERVED

TRIP:	DATE: / /

LOCATION(S):

IMPRESSION(S):

NOTES/MAPS/SKETCHES:

☐ OBSERVED

OBSERVATIONS

TRIP: | DATE: / /

LOCATION(S):

IMPRESSION(S):

NOTES/MAPS/SKETCHES:

☐ OBSERVED

TRIP: _____ DATE: ___ / ___ / ___

LOCATION(S):

_____

_____

_____

_____

_____

IMPRESSION(S):

_____

_____

_____

_____

_____

_____

NOTES/MAPS/SKETCHES:

☐ OBSERVED

OBSERVATIONS

TRIP:	DATE: / /

LOCATION(S):

IMPRESSION(S):

NOTES/MAPS/SKETCHES:

☐ OBSERVED

TRIP: | DATE: / /

LOCATION(S):

_____

_____

_____

_____

_____

IMPRESSION(S):

_____

_____

_____

_____

_____

_____

NOTES/MAPS/SKETCHES:

☐ OBSERVED

OBSERVATIONS

TRIP:	DATE: / /

LOCATION(S):

IMPRESSION(S):

NOTES/MAPS/SKETCHES:

☐ OBSERVED

TRIP: | DATE: / /

LOCATION(S):

IMPRESSION(S):

NOTES/MAPS/SKETCHES:

☐ OBSERVED

OBSERVATIONS

TRIP:	DATE: / /

LOCATION(S):

IMPRESSION(S):

NOTES/MAPS/SKETCHES:

☐ OBSERVED

TRIP:	DATE: / /

LOCATION(S):

IMPRESSION(S):

NOTES/MAPS/SKETCHES:

☐ OBSERVED

OBSERVATIONS

TRIP:	DATE: / /

LOCATION(S):

IMPRESSION(S):

NOTES/MAPS/SKETCHES:

☐ OBSERVED

TRIP: DATE: /   /

LOCATION(S):

IMPRESSION(S):

NOTES/MAPS/SKETCHES:

☐ OBSERVED

OBSERVATIONS

TRIP: | DATE: /   /

LOCATION(S):

IMPRESSION(S):

NOTES/MAPS/SKETCHES:

☐ OBSERVED

TRIP: | DATE: / /

LOCATION(S):

IMPRESSION(S):

NOTES/MAPS/SKETCHES:

☐ OBSERVED

OBSERVATIONS

TRIP:	DATE: / /

LOCATION(S):

IMPRESSION(S):

NOTES/MAPS/SKETCHES:

□ OBSERVED

TRIP: **DATE:**   /   /

LOCATION(S):

IMPRESSION(S):

NOTES/MAPS/SKETCHES:

☐ OBSERVED

OBSERVATIONS

TRIP:	DATE: / /

LOCATION(S):

IMPRESSION(S):

NOTES/MAPS/SKETCHES:

☐ OBSERVED

TRIP: | DATE: / /

LOCATION(S):

IMPRESSION(S):

NOTES/MAPS/SKETCHES:

☐ OBSERVED

OBSERVATIONS

TRIP:	DATE: / /

LOCATION(S):

IMPRESSION(S):

NOTES/MAPS/SKETCHES:

☐ OBSERVED

TRIP: **DATE:**   /   /

LOCATION(S):

IMPRESSION(S):

NOTES/MAPS/SKETCHES:

☐ OBSERVED

OBSERVATIONS

TRIP:	DATE: / /

LOCATION(S):

IMPRESSION(S):

NOTES/MAPS/SKETCHES:

☐ OBSERVED

TRIP: **DATE:**   /   /

LOCATION(S):

IMPRESSION(S):

NOTES/MAPS/SKETCHES:

☐ OBSERVED

OBSERVATIONS

TRIP:	DATE: / /

LOCATION(S):

IMPRESSION(S):

NOTES/MAPS/SKETCHES:

☐ OBSERVED

TRIP: **DATE:**   /   /

LOCATION(S):

IMPRESSION(S):

NOTES/MAPS/SKETCHES:

☐ OBSERVED

OBSERVATIONS

TRIP:	DATE: / /

LOCATION(S):

IMPRESSION(S):

NOTES/MAPS/SKETCHES:

☐ OBSERVED

TRIP: _____ DATE: ___ / ___ / ___

LOCATION(S):

_____

_____

_____

_____

_____

_____

IMPRESSION(S):

_____

_____

_____

_____

_____

_____

_____

NOTES/MAPS/SKETCHES:

☐ OBSERVED

OBSERVATIONS

TRIP:	DATE: / /

LOCATION(S):

IMPRESSION(S):

NOTES/MAPS/SKETCHES:

☐ OBSERVED

TRIP: | DATE: / /

LOCATION(S):

IMPRESSION(S):

NOTES/MAPS/SKETCHES:

☐ OBSERVED

OBSERVATIONS

TRIP:	DATE: / /

LOCATION(S):

IMPRESSION(S):

NOTES/MAPS/SKETCHES:

☐ OBSERVED

TRIP:	DATE: / /

LOCATION(S):

IMPRESSION(S):

NOTES/MAPS/SKETCHES:

☐ OBSERVED

OBSERVATIONS

TRIP:	DATE: / /

LOCATION(S):

IMPRESSION(S):

NOTES/MAPS/SKETCHES:

☐ OBSERVED

TRIP: _____ DATE: _____ / _____ / _____

LOCATION(S): _____

_____

_____

_____

_____

_____

IMPRESSION(S): _____

_____

_____

_____

_____

_____

_____

NOTES/MAPS/SKETCHES:

☐ OBSERVED

REFERENCE

EXTREMELY IMPORTANT, OFTEN-FORGOTTEN ITEMS

Passport / ID

Confirmation numbers for travel and lodging

Money / credit card(s)

Insurance info

Phone

Charger(s)

Medication

Sunscreen

Glasses / contact lenses / sunglasses

Plug adaptors

Camera / extra memory cards or film

...AND DON'T FORGET TO

Check passport expiration date

Leave copies of itinerary, passport, ID, and credit card(s) with trusted person

Alert credit card companies of travel plans

Pay bills

Arrange for mail / newspaper pickup or suspension

Orient sitters / caretakers

Confirm reservations

Forward email or set up auto-response

Unplug power-surge-sensitive appliances

Remove perishables from refrigerator

Set timer(s) / alarm(s)

Lock windows and door(s)

HOW TO SAY HELLO AND GOODBYE IN NINE POPULAR LANGUAGES

LANGUAGE	HELLO	GOODBYE
French	Bonjour (boh(n)-zhur)	Au revoir (oh ruh-VWAHR)
German	Guten Tag (GOO-ten tahk)	Auf Wiedersehen (owf VEE-der-zay-en)
Greek	Yassas (YAH-sahss)	Andio (AHN-dee-oh)
Italian	Buon giorno (bwohn JOHR-noh)	Arrivederla (ahr-ree-veh-DEHR-lah)
Japanese	Konnichiwa (kon-nee-chee-wah)	Sayōnara (sa-YOHH-nah-rah)
Mandarin	Nǐ hǎo (KNEE how)	Zài jiàn (ZYE jeeyen)
Russian	Zdravstvuyte (ZDRAHST-vooy-tyeh)	Do svidanja (duh svee-DAH-nyah)
Spanish	Hola (OH-lah)	Adiós (ah-DYOHS)
American Sign Language		

HOW TO SAY PLEASE AND THANK YOU IN NINE POPULAR LANGUAGES

LANGUAGE	PLEASE	THANK YOU
French	S'il vous plaît (SEEL voo PLEH)	Merci (mehr-SEE)
German	Bitte (BIT-tuh)	Danke (DAN-keh)
Greek	Parakalo (pah-rah-kah-LOH)	Efharisto (ef-hah-rees-TOH)
Italian	Per favore (PEHR fah-VOH-reh)	Grazie (GRAHT-tsyeh)
Japanese	Kudasai (koo-dah-sah-ee)	Arigatō (ah-ree-GAH-toh)
Mandarin	Qǐng (ching)	Xièxiè (SHE-ay-she-ay)
Russian	Pozhaluysta (pah-ZHAH-luh-stuh)	Spasibo (spuh-SEE-buh)
Spanish	Por favor (POHR fah-VOHR)	Gracias (GRAH-syahs)
American Sign Language		

Usage and spelling may vary due to differences in alphabet, dialect, and custom.

CURRENCY NAMES AROUND THE WORLD

Country	Currency	Country	Currency
Argentina	Peso	Malaysia	Ringgit
Australia	Dollar	Mexico	Peso
Brazil	Real	Morocco	Dirham
Bulgaria	Lev	New Zealand	Dollar
Canada	Dollar	Norway	Krone
Chile	Peso	Pakistan	Rupee
China	Yuan renminbi	Peru	Nuevo sol
Colombia	Peso	Philippines	Peso
Croatia	Kuna	Poland	Zloty
Czech Republic	Koruna	Romania	Leu
Denmark	Krone	Russia	Ruble
Dominican Republic	Peso	Saudi Arabia	Riyal
Egypt	Pound	Singapore	Dollar
European Union	Euro	South Africa	Rand
Hong Kong	Dollar	South Korea	Won
Hungary	Forint	Sweden	Krona
India	Rupee	Switzerland	Franc
Indonesia	Rupiah	Thailand	Baht
Iraq	Dinar	Turkey	Lira
Israel	New shekel	United Arab Emirates	Dirham
Japan	Yen	United Kingdom	Pound
Jordan	Dinar	United States	Dollar
Kuwait	Dinar	Vietnam	Dong

Currency that shares name may not share value.

NOTES